Songs for Dancing
Creative Movement Activities for Children

Kate Kuper
With music by Neal Robinson

Music and Arrangements: Neal Robinson
Lyrics and Songs: Kate Kuper
Executive Producer: Rocky Maffit
Cover Design: Kati Hufford
Book Design: WordStreamCopy
Videographer/Editor of DVD: Bill Yauch, Rielly Boy Productions
Editor: Jeanette Morgan

Permission-to-Reproduce Notice
Permission to photocopy the visual aids in this product is hereby granted to one teacher as part of the purchase price. This permission may not be transferred, sold, or given to any additional or subsequent user of this product. If you are interested in licensing the product for use by multiple teachers within your facility, please contact our permissions department at (800) 444-1144 x1. Thank you for respecting the copyright laws.
© 2012 Heritage Music Press, a division of The Lorenz Corporation, and its licensors. All rights reserved.
Heritage Music Press
A division of The Lorenz Corporation
PO Box 802
Dayton OH 45401
www.lorenz.com
Printed in the United States of America
ISBN: 978-1-4291-2680-9

HERITAGE MUSIC PRESS
A Lorenz Company • www.lorenz.com

OPUS II
100 Ahrens St. West
Kitchener N2H 4C3
Phone 519-743-4362

*To the memory of my parents, Alan and Ginger,
who encouraged and supported a life of creative expression.*

Foreword

Songs for Dancing is a collection of original and traditional music and movement activities for children ages two to eight. It reflects my thirty years of teaching dance to preschool and primary-aged children in school and studio settings. The CD has many guided tracks that include voice prompts. These are followed by instrumental tracks that have no sung or spoken accompaniment and can be used at your discretion. In this way, you can either follow along with me or invent your own ways of working with the music. In the DVD, I model clear expectations for behavior and lots of positive reinforcement, give detailed front-loading of the activities, and demonstrate many opportunities for children to make creative choices. By using the DVD as a practice tool for your own teaching, you will become a confident activity leader.

Enjoy your journey through this material. As you become comfortable with instructing the activities, feel free to use your own creativity to alter them and make the lessons your own. I hope that each piece finds a special place in your instruction for years to come.

Kate Kuper

Contents

About this Resource 4
About the CD and DVD 6
Connecting to Curriculum 8

Down by the Station... 9
The Welcome Song 11
Flea Song... 14
Everybody Do This.. 16
Shape Song 22
Do Your Own Dance 27
Right and Left Hands 29
Galloping Song 31
Skipping Song 33
Walking Song 35
Here We Go 'Round and 'Round 38
A Trip to the Zoo 41
Popcorn and Melted Butter... 45
Old MacDonald Had a Farm 47
Free Dance 48
Little Birdies 49
Resting 52
Goodbye Song 53

Body Shapes for Learning 55
Lesson Plan Suggestions 56
Early Childhood Concept Index 57
Quick Reference Guide.. 60

About this Resource

All of the activities presented in this book can be taught to preschool and primary students. I've organized the first activities, from "Down by the Station" through "Everybody Do This," as activities appropriate for the beginning of a movement class. The next set of activities, through "Free Dance," should be selected based on your lesson objectives. "Little Birdies" and "Resting" are quiet activities, which can serve as transitions towards reflection or as refreshing breaks between more active segments. "Goodbye Song" can serve as a closure activity and a transition out of the space or be useful at other times of the day or year.

The lessons are presented in the following format:

- ★ Objectives: state the intended outcomes of the activity
- ★ Activity Basics: provide the step-by-step lesson suggestions that match the activities as presented on the DVD
- ★ Going Further: provides additional details for instruction and extension ideas
- ★ Reflection: provides closure and a means of assessing your objectives
- ★ Concepts for Dance, Music, Physical Education, and Early Childhood
- ★ Lyrics

The sidebar includes CD track information, DVD Options, DVD Commentary, and information about visual resources available on the mixed-media CD.

Throughout the book you will see this icon:

It highlights phrases, tips, and tricks that I use in my everyday instruction.

When you conduct reflection and closure, encourage students to either show (good for kinesthetic learners) or tell (good for verbal learners) in response to reflection questions. This will draw out the non-verbal learners as demonstrators. It will also provide the verbal learners with opportunities to express (in words) what they see modeled (in movement) by a peer.

A word about front-loading

Front-loading means "to concentrate maximum effort (on an activity) at the outset." Front-loading reveals the activity road map, helping children confidently assume ownership of their movement experience. It clears up misunderstandings and helps minimize the need to backtrack. Use front-loading to clarify movements, interactions, and transitions within an activity. Select the fewest, best points. Then, layer on additional details as children move and dance.

Be sure to front-load musically. When a song and dance go together, I often sing the melody with my own instructing words. This helps children experience the structure of the activity and anticipate the transitions before they even hear the music.

You may find it easier to understand how to front-load an activity for the children if you view an activity on the DVD and read the notes in this book at the same time.

A word about movement terminology

There are different ways to describe movement that is performed in place and that which travels through a space. For the most part, I will use the words non-locomotor and locomotor, respectively, to differentiate these two ways of moving, following the National Standards for Dance (1996). In addition to non-locomotor, in-place movement is also called stationary, axial, personal, or self-space movement. Traveling movement is also called movement through the general (group, shared) space.

Gross motor skills suggest large movement of the limbs and whole body. Fine motor skills suggest small movements of the hands, wrists, fingers, feet, toes, lips, and tongue. Both can be practiced in-place or traveling.

About the CD and DVD

The CD included in this product is enhanced and contains both audio tracks and digital files to assist you in presenting these activities to your students. The CD will play audio files like any regular CD in your CD player. To access the digital files, you will need a PDF reader, such as Adobe Reader, which you can download for free at http://get.adobe.com/reader/. Once you have installed a PDF reader, simply insert your CD into your computer's CD drive. When prompted, click on **View Files** to see the resources available to you.

Digital Files include:

- ★ Lyrics for most songs
- ★ Visuals for "Shape Song"
- ★ Visuals for "A Trip to the Zoo"
- ★ Visuals for "Here We Go 'Round and 'Round"
- ★ Visuals for "Walking Song"

Each dance activity includes two audio tracks: a guided track and an instrumental track. The guided tracks have voice prompts for the dance, while the instrumental tracks are just the instruments. Feel free to use the instrumental tracks for other purposes beyond *Songs for Dancing*.

The DVD is designed solely for the instructor's eyes and instruction, with one exception. Watch the "Old MacDonald" video together and have fun.

Watch the video demonstrations on the DVD to learn how to conduct in-depth front-loading before you teach an activity the first time. This will also help you to choose age-appropriate versions and practice the script and sequence. The modeling on the DVD is authentic. Students, ages 4–7, were familiar with the studio space but had never been together in that particular grouping and were new to most of the activities. Though no boys appear in the DVD, boys *do* dance, and should be encouraged at every opportunity!

Each dance has its own menu from which you can select the parts that you would like to review.

Don't miss the Tips and Tricks section of the DVD in which I model valuable classroom management strategies. You will see many of these tips embedded in the activities. However, some segments are exclusive to the Tips and Tricks section, and you will want to take the time to review these helpful strategies. You'll also find these tips useful in other contexts, such as during transition times.

This section includes the following choices:

- ★ Body Shapes for Learning
- ★ Mind and Body: A few things to think about
- ★ Self, General, and Empty Space
- ★ Soft Focus
- ★ Making a Line: Two examples
- ★ Making a Circle: Three examples
- ★ Mountain Breathing
- ★ "I see…."
- ★ One, Two, Three, Transition!
- ★ Changing Heads
- ★ Concentration Dust
- ★ Separating Whispering Partners

Connecting to Curriculum

Early Learning Standards

All of the activities in *Songs for Dancing* address the following Early Learning Standards:

Language Arts

Listen with understanding and respond to directions

Physical Development

Engage in active play using gross motor skills

Follow rules and procedures when participating in group physical activity

Participate in activities that promote healthy living

Fine Arts

Investigate the elements of dance

Use creative arts as an avenue for self-expression

Social and Emotional Development

Begin to understand and follow rules

Engage in cooperative group play

Early Childhood concepts are covered for each activity in greater detail in the Early Childhood Concept Index, beginning on page 57.

More Ideas

You can strengthen children's expression in writing and drawing through extension activities. Draw and write impressions of the music and dance during table time. Write dictated captions for the drawings or have children write their own.

Decorate your room or hallway with dancing shapes by tracing children's body shapes on butcher paper. Cut out the shapes and display them. This helps reinforce shape concepts and makes attractive and lively wall art.

Graph favorite dances using written or picture language (such as a drawing of a locomotive train for "Down by the Station," a triangle and a square for "Shape Song," or a bird for "Little Birdies"). Use tally marks under each picture to indicate favorites.

Down by the Station

This is a great piece to begin class and move your students to the activity area. You can also end class with this song to move to the door or the next activity area—even from room to room!

Objectives
★ To help children travel in a moving line
★ To engage the imagination

Activity Basics
1. Teach the train moves by modeling the arm movements first.
2. Model the leg movements separately.
3. Put them together.
4. Practice the "chug, whoo, whoo" sounds and gesture as a group.
5. Discover that the head of the train is the locomotive.
6. Assign the first child behind the leader (locomotive) as the coal car. The last child is the caboose. Assign cars to everyone else, such as passenger, box, flat, hopper, and tanker. If you wish, embellish this process by saying things like "You are a tanker carrying pink lemonade," or "You are a box car carrying stuffed animals." I often take time with this on the first day of the activity to help activate imagination.
7. Remind the cars to stay one behind the other.
8. Play the guided CD track, moving about the room as demonstrated on the DVD.

Going Further
★ Play with dramatic possibilities by exploring the "open country." Point, scan the horizon, call out names of animals or plants you see, etc.

Reflection
Ask your students:
★ What kind of train car were you?
★ How did you travel (locomote)? (Walk, shuffle)
★ How did you move your hands? Your feet?
★ What shapes did the group make? (Line, curving line, circle)

CD Tracks
① Guided
㉒ Instrumental

DVD Options
- Instruction & Demonstration
- Demonstration

DVD Commentary
The Instruction & Demonstration segment provides many strategies for introducing the activity and extension ideas to try in future repetitions.

The Demonstration segment shows the activity in full, without screen tips, so you can concentrate on the uninterrupted flow.

Concepts

Dance	*Music*	*Physical Education*	*Early Childhood*
Space: pathways	Steady beat	**Space:** pathways	Physical Development
Time: pulse		Social behavior	

Down by the Station

Down by the station, early in the morning,

See the little pufferbillies, all in a row.

See the stationmaster, pull the little handle.

Chug, chug, whoo, whoo!

Off we go!

The Welcome Song

Objectives

★ To begin movement activities and get acquainted

★ To familiarize children with working in a standing circle

★ To explore in-place movement and body shapes

★ To engage in critical thinking

★ To practice sequence and recall

Activity Basics

1. Form a seated circle.

2. Wave hello and tell the children that you have a fancy word for hello. The word is *welcome*. Using echo imitation, have the children wave too, without speaking.

3. Now, wave with two hands and one foot to show that this is not your typical hello wave!

4. Wave with different body parts: two feet, both elbows, nose, shoulders, and knees.

5. Wave on different levels: up high; down low; next to your ears, like Dumbo!

6. Wave in different spaces around your body: above your head; do a secret wave behind your back; wave under one arm; under one leg; the other leg; two hands under both legs; under your chin; beside yourself!

7. Now, choose one or more silly ways of waving and perform it/them as the song plays during "Welcome, welcome everyone." Lead the students in the movements as discussed below and seen on the video as the song plays:

    - For "touch the sun," brainstorm with the children. Ask, "Where is the sun? How could we get closer to it? (Stand up!) Even closer? (Jump, climb, reach!) Let's jump on the words 'touch the sun.'" Ask, "How many jumps? (Three! After all, the sun is 93,000,000 miles away and we have to get up high to touch it!)"

    - For "now let's make the rain fall down, gently, gently, to the ground," twinkle your fingers in an S-curve as you move from high to low.

    - For "close yourself into a ball," crouch down.

    - At the end of the song, jump up tall raising your arms and stretching your body.

CD Tracks
② Guided
㉓ Instrumental

DVD Options
- Instruction & Demonstration
- Demonstration

DVD Commentary
See page 12

Going Further

★ Ask for funny waves from your students each time you do the dance, and pick one to three different ideas each time.

★ Dance on your spot in the circle.

 Bodies move, mouths don't! (Unless you are singing the song.)

★ Ask for rhyming words with the "all" sound, like ball or tall, and jump up into a shape that shows the rhyming word idea. Examples:

> Wall: jump into a wide shape
>
> Shopping mall: jump into a square shape
>
> Call: jump to a gesture shape to show call (on the phone, or between your hands)

Other fun morpheme combinations are sprawl, crawl, shawl, Paul (a boy), and Saul (a king).

Reflection

Ask your students:

★ What parts of our body did we use to wave hello?

★ When did we make a high shape? A low shape?

★ When did we move slowly? (Melting down on "rain.") Quickly? (Jumping up on "tall.")

★ Show one way we jumped up from a ball shape. What was the word that sounded like ball?

DVD Commentary

Notice how I use active listening when working with the children. As they offer spontaneous creative ideas, I listen and either use their ideas without modifications or redirect them into more appropriate and productive directions. In this way, I control the outcome and still construct the learning experience with the students. This is also true when we work on rhyming words at the end of the activity. One child suggests we fall, and I direct it into a slow motion fall. I could have offered a choice to the children ("Would you like to fall slowly or quickly?") to differentiate for learners with different temperaments. As the leader, you need to read the situation and determine which choices will be appropriate given the children's ages, their level of self-control, and their social competence.

Notice how we balance on one leg for a very short time when standing and waving under the other leg. Go for it … and keep it brief. The same applies to big jumps, spins, and other dynamic movements.

Notice how I name the different waves that children offer. Using hearing as well as seeing helps us keep the sequence in our minds. The demonstration waves are "swinging," "twisting," and "shaking." They could also be named for emotions (happy wave), shapes (straight wave), size (giant wave), location (under wave), or other defining characteristics.

Steer the children into offering variations, rather than outright rejecting an identical suggestion. In the demonstration, one child shows a swing and the second a very similar swing, which I direct into a twist. This models building upon ideas and helps the children be courageous about offering their thoughts without fear of rejection.

Concepts

Dance
Space: self-space, levels, pathways (air)

Body: parts, shapes

Gesture

Music
Singing

Pulse

Physical Education
Body: parts

Early Childhood
Language Arts

Math

Physical Development

Social & Emotional Development

The Welcome Song

Welcome, welcome, everyone.

Let's reach up and touch the sun.

Now let's make the rain fall down,

Gently, gently to the ground.

Close yourself into a ball,

One, two, three, let's jump up tall!

Flea Song

CD Tracks
- ③ Guided
- ㉔ Instrumental

DVD Options
- Instruction & Demonstration
- Seated version
- Standing version

DVD Commentary

Notice how I model the "legs like number eleven" shape, using visual reinforcement to indicate the two lines.

When standing during the tactile sections, feel free to touch more than just the front surface of the body. I model touching on the back and sides, as well as the front in the standing version.

Objectives
★ To participate in a tactile warm up or cool down
★ To stretch the back, and back of the legs

Activity Basics

1. Start in a seated circle, soles of the feet facing to the center, legs long and extended.

    Legs make two straight lines, like the number eleven.

2. Play the guided CD track. Demonstrate how to take time to touch the toes without bending the knees. Let passive weight work for you. The song opens with an introduction to help you do just that. Keep your shoulders wide and relaxed.

3. Starting at the toes, walk (or squeeze, pat, scratch, and brush, following the prompts on the guided CD track) your fingers up to the top of your head and back down again. Pass your stomach and nose on the way up. Pass your stomach and knees on the way down.

4. Slap your toes on "take that you flea!" Wag your finger at the flea, too!

Going Further
★ Perform the whole dance standing, bending to touch your toes, working up the body and down. In the standing version, you can easily include tactile movement on the sides and back of the body.
★ Use the instrumental track to sing a traditional version, replacing the tactile words with "climbing" or other tactile words, such as slapping, pinching, and tapping.

Reflection

Discuss the following questions with your students:
★ What does tactile mean? (Touch)
★ What were some ways we used touch when the flea climbed up and down?
★ Where is your stomach? Nose? Where are your knees?

Concepts

Dance	*Music*	*Physical Education*	*Early Childhood*
Body: parts	Expression	**Body:** parts	Physical Development
Direction	Steady Beat		
Energy			

Flea Song

Stretch your arms and legs, breathe in through your nose.
Bend yourself forward to touch your toes.
Breathe in deep, in through your nose.
Bend yourself forward to touch your toes.

On my toe there is a flea,
Now he's squeezing up on me,
Past my stomach, past my nose,
On my head where my hair grows.

On my head there is a flea,
Now he's patting down on me,
Past my stomach, past my knees,
On my toe … take THAT you flea!

On my toe there is a flea,
Now he's scratching up on me,
Past my stomach, past my nose,
On my head where my hair grows.

On my head there is a flea,
Now he's brushing down on me,
Past my stomach, past my knees,
On my toe … take THAT you flea!

Everybody Do This

CD Tracks
4–7 Guided
25–28 Instrumental

DVD Option
- Instruction & Demonstration

DVD Commentary
See page 19

This is a group of four, short tracks. Track 4 is a sequence of four different movement ideas, each 16 beats long. Track 5 is a repetition of the previous track, but each sequence only lasts 8 beats. Tracks 6 and 7 follow the same pattern with a different set of four movement ideas. Teach one sequence and repetition (Tracks 4 and 5 or Tracks 6 and 7) on a given day.

In the guided version of the song, I provide voice prompts several beats before the changes, anticipating the transition to the next movement while in the midst of doing the current movement. I call this "being in the present and a little in the future." Incorporating this strategy will help your dancers to transition smoothly and in time.

Objectives

★ To practice sequence and recall
★ To warm up for movement

Preparation

Before you teach this song, listen to the song and note the tempo and structure of the piece. There are two sections, one with 16 beats and one with 8 beats. Dancers often think of 16 beats as four sets of four beats. Musicians often think of it as four bars in $\frac{4}{4}$ time. You can also think of it as 1, 2, 3, 4; 1, 2, 3, 4; 1, 2, 3, 4; 1, 2, 3, 4. The eight-beat section can be broken down and discussed in similar ways.

Practice cueing (signaling) transitions. In this activity, you will lead four transitions from one movement pattern to the next. With the action sequence written down in front of you or memorized, practice saying, "Now we're going to change to the _____ thing." (clapping, jumping, twisting, flapping or first, second, third, fourth). You should say this phrase rhythmically over the course of the 4 beats before the transition happens. Listen to the guided CD track or watch the video for further clarification.

Action Sequence Suggestions

Tracks 4 and 5

1. Clap your hands
2. Tilt your head from side to side
3. Flap your elbows like a chicken
4. Bounce your body up and down

OR

1. Shrug your shoulders up and down
2. Tip your whole body side to side, like a teeter-totter
3. Knock your knees together
4. Jump a directional pattern: forward/home/backward/home

Tracks 6 and 7

1. Twist your waist
2. March in place
3. Yawn and stretch … fall asleep and droop over … pop up to wake up!
4. Fold your arms and kick your legs forward, like a Russian dancer

OR

1. Swing your arms in a twisty way from one side to the other
2. March forward 4 steps, backwards 4 steps
3. Slowly, twinkle your fingers around in a big circle one way and then the other
4. Do small jumping jacks or crisscross legs with hands on hips

Activity Basics

1. Prepare your students to get ready to use their memories by using the following script, if you wish:

   I'm going to ask you to remember four things. But I'm not going to ask you to remember anything else we've done before this. So we are going to need a new head. Pop! Off comes your head. Set it down behind you. Take a new head from the pile in front. Put it on. Check your neck. Is your hair all there? Is your chin in? Do you have an ear here, and here?

   With this new head you are going to remember… how many? Four things! After we do them, I'm going to ask you what we did.

2. Play the song.

3. Choose actions from Action Sequence Suggestions to perform. Each sequence takes 16 beats. Move with the pulse of the music. Cue the transition during the last 4 beats of each section, before the transition occurs.

4. Stop and review what you did, asking the children to recall the actions and the action sequence.

5. Using the next track on the CD, repeat the four actions for half as long (8 beats). Remember to cue the transition during the last 4 beats of each section.

6. Change back to your old head, using the following script, if you wish:

 Time to change back to your regular head. Take off your new head. Get your old head and put it on. Is your face in place? Does your nose know where it goes? Do the eyes have it? Have you got your forehead? Gums? The bridge of your nose? Eyelashes?

Going Further

★ From older children, ask for the order in which you did the motions/actions. For younger, just ask them to remember any of the four things.

★ Visual learning strategy: Hold up four fingers when you teach "four things."

★ Auditory learning strategy: During recall, sing the song's melody with the lyrics, "If you can remember / what the first thing was / raise your hand and then I'll / call on you." When you get to "you," select a child to share their response.

★ For a higher challenge level, vary the direction, speed, or relationship of the movement during one, sixteen-beat pattern. For example, instead of simply clapping in front of yourself sixteen times, clap high, low, side right, and side left (either four times each or two times each and then repeat the pattern).

★ For a lower level of difficulty, ask for recall without accurate sequencing and provide visual and auditory cues (saying things such as "we used our hands," or "the music said 'tick-tock.'")

★ Use the instrumental tracks to invent your own movements.

★ In later repetitions, or when singing without accompaniment, pass leadership for a movement idea to different children, singing "just like (child's name)."

Reflection

Ask your students:

- ★ What actions used the "tw" sound? (Twist, twinkle) The "m" sound? (March, melt) The "s" sound? (Spin, stretch)
- ★ What actions used hands? Feet? Waist?
- ★ What actions were slow? Fast?
- ★ What actions changed levels? (From high to low, or low to high)

DVD Commentary

Notice how I hold up four fingers to provide visual support. I also prompt the students to say the ordinal numbers as I count them on my fingers. The combination of seeing and hearing is a powerful teaching tool.

"New heads" help children differentiate activities. Notice how one child mentions something we did previously and I say, "That was with our old heads." Head changes are a great way to name and locate different parts of the head and face, including the little detailed parts like eyebrows, foreheads, and gums!

Remember to teach and repeat only one sequence during an activity session.

Notice how the circle shrinks when the children do the Russian kicks. Knowing that this is typical, you can disaster-proof the moment by opening up the circle and reminding your students to stay on their spots. This is also a chance for you to move between your most spirited students and help them maintain distance by using your proximity and "The Look." You know the one I mean.

Concepts

Dance	Music	Physical Education	Early Childhood
Space: levels, direction	Steady Beat	Moving to a steady beat	Language Arts
Body: parts	Form	Demonstrate and describe movements in a sequence	Physical Development
Time: pulse			Math
Demonstrate and describe movements in a sequence			Social Science

Everybody Do This (First set)

Let's do four things, and then remember what we've done.
Everybody do this, do this, do this,
Everybody do this, just like me. (Repeat)

Ticka-ticka-tick-tock, tick-tock, tick-tock,
Ticka-ticka-tick-tock, just like me. (Repeat)

Bucka-bucka, buck-buck, buck-buck, buck-buck,
Bucka-bucka, buck b'gee! Just like me. (Repeat)

Boinga-boinga, boing-boing, boing-boing, boing-boing,
Boinga-boinga, boing-boing, just like me. (Repeat)

Now, we'll repeat our four things.
Everybody do this, do this, do this,
Everybody do this, just like me.

Ticka-ticka, tick-tock, tick-tock, tick-tock,
Ticka-ticka, tick-tock, just like me.

Bucka-bucka, buck-buck, buck-buck, buck-buck,
Bucka-bucka, buck b'gee! Just like me.

Boinga-boinga-boing-boing, boing-boing, boing-boing,
Boinga, boinga, boing-boing, just like me.

Everybody Do This (Second set)

Here are four things to do and remember.

Twist-a, twist-a—twisting, twisting, twisting
Twist-a, twist-a, twisting, just like me. (Repeat)

March-a, march-a—marching, marching, marching
March-a, march-a, marching, just like me. (Repeat)

Everybody stretch and yawn–a, yawn–a
Droop-a, droop-a, sleep-a, just like me! (Repeat)

Everybody do this, do this, do this,
Everybody do this, just like me. (Repeat)

Let's repeat our four things.

Twist-a, twist-a—twisting, twisting, twisting
Twist-a, twist-a, twisting, just like me.

March-a, march-a—marching, marching, marching
March-a, march-a— marching, just like me.

Everybody stretch and yawn–a, yawn–a
Droop-a, droop-a, sleep-a , just like me!

Everybody do this, do this, do this,
Everybody do this, just like me.

Shape Song

CD Tracks
 Guided
㉙ Instrumental

DVD Options
- Exploring shapes
- First verse
- Second verse
- Demonstration

DVD Commentary
See page 25

Picture Sequence Visual (available on the CD)

Objectives
★ To explore body shapes
★ To practice sequence and recall

Activity Basics

1. Model the four shapes as children follow along:

   Tall as a tree: stretch and reach up

   Wide as a house: stretch and reach laterally, with legs wider and bent

   Thin as a needle: bring your limbs in, make yourself narrow, arms high or low

   Small as a mouse: crouch

2. Repeat the sequence one or more times. Consider making more shapes. See Going Further.

3. Display the Picture Sequence Visual of the song (available as a digital file on the CD), and point out each part. Sing the song with the children and again point out each part.

4. Teach the middle of verse one first. This is the straight line/triangle shape/tiny box sequence. Teach as follows:

   - Make a reaching-up straight line.
   - Bend forward at the hip joint and walk your hands (not your feet) forward three times so that your arms and legs are stretching to (and touching) the floor, and the hips stay high. (I count the hand steps with the phrase "One, two, three!")

    Get your belly button up high!

22 ★ Shape Song

- Bend your knees to the floor to create a square (or rectangle) shape (the "tiny box").

5. Reverse the sequence:
   - Tuck your toes under and get your belly button up high to make the triangle again.
   - Walk your hands back ("One, two, three!") and hands walk up the imaginary wall in front of you, leaving big handprints, until you are a straight line again.

6. Practice moving between these three shapes. This is an excellent spine and whole-body stretch!

7. Add movements for the "sun up" and "flower up" parts to the sequence:
   - Begin with an empty-space circle in front of you (the sun) and bring it from low to high. This transitions out of the "small as a mouse" shape, when children are in a low crouch.
   - For the flower growing, rise up in a curving pathway from low to high (like time-lapse photography of a flower growing). Children can invent their own ways to grow, too. End in an open shape.

8. Sequence the whole first verse.

9. Teach verse two. Have the students sit in ready position, facing the chart.

10. Have the students explore ways to create three triangles using their bodies. To front-load, have the students stand with legs apart and ask them, "Do you see one triangle?" (It's under the legs.) Instruct them to then "Add one hand on one hip" and ask, "Do you see two triangles?" (One is under the legs; the other is in the empty space of the arm). Finally, instruct them to add a hand on their heads. Ask, "Do you see three triangles?" Switch hands and ask, "Do you still see three triangles?" Invite your students to explore other ways to make triangles. Have the students count the triangles they see in other shapes. Here are some shapes to try:

    - Superman/Superwoman: Hands on hips, legs apart
    - I'm A Little Teapot: Hand on hip, hand on head, legs apart
    - Tree: Balance on one leg, with one foot on the inner knee of the standing leg, hands on hips
    - Egyptian: Legs apart in the front/back direction, hands on back and front, elbows pointing back and front

11. Invite the students to make a crazy shape! For a challenge, try balancing on one leg for the crazy shape.

12. Play with changing from "three triangles" to "crazy shapes" several times.

13. Teach the sun goes down (Your arms form an empty circle that goes from high to low) and spin yourself around (one spin!). For a challenge, spin in a bent over shape and pop-up straight to make your three triangles shape.

14. Add the crazy shape and melting like ice cream.

15. Sequence the second verse.

16. Play the recording and perform the whole song from the beginning.

Going Further

★ After you have made the tall, wide, thin, and small shapes and before you introduce "Shape Song," consider exploring some more shapes. Here are some ideas:
- As flat as a pancake (pour on syrup!)
- As round as a ball
- As twisted as a bent piece of wire or a pretzel
- As straight as a number one (lying down or standing up)
- As curved as the letter "S" (remember it has two curves)
- With three sides and three corners like a … triangle
- With four sides and four corners like a … square, rectangle, or diamond

Describe your observations to encourage a variety of solutions to the creative problem and use "I see…." (e.g. "I see round shapes with people crouched low, lying on their sides, on their backs.") Use your voice, a clap, or drumbeat to cue moving and then freezing in shapes.

★ For the "Shape Song," gather ideas for "growing" and "melting" and change the lyrics to match. Examples are "grow up like a corn stalk" or "melt like the Wicked Witch."

★ While in transition from the four shapes to the first verse at the beginning of "Shape Song," I say, "Wiggle your mousie ears, your mousie nose, and your mousie tail" to fill the time before making the sun shape with your arms.

★ Use the Picture Sequence Visual to visually cue the sequence.

Reflection

Discuss what kinds of shapes your students made, being sure to engage all in the discussion.

DVD Commentary

Notice how I work from simple to more complex as I introduce different shapes in the "Exploring Shapes" segment. At first, the children make straight and round shapes. They graduate to the "S" curve. Then I introduce the idea of "three sides and three corners" to encourage critical thinking so that the children will discover the triangle shapes themselves. Next, I introduce the idea of solving a shape problem (square or rectangle) with another person, after they have processed the exploration by themselves. This more complex layer of relating adds the challenge of problem solving and communicating with another person, a task that children will need to do many times in their lives to become socially competent.

Observe how I balance instruction time with movement time. There is a great deal of front-loading in this activity. When children become excited about doing something, such as spinning one time in the "Second Verse" segment, it pays to allow the students a moment to spin, rather than delaying their gratification. I follow this impulse when children initiate interest, verbally or physically, and then quickly redirect. In this way, they can concentrate on the next part of the sequence instead of being distracted or frustrated by the thing they didn't get to do.

Concepts

Dance
Body: shapes
Space: self space, level
Demonstrate and describe movements in a sequence
Making connections between dance and math

Music
Introduction
Verse

Physical Education
Body: shapes
Demonstrate and describe movements in a sequence

Early Childhood
Language Arts
Math
Physical Development
Social & Emotional Development

Shape Song

Tall as a tree
Wide as a house
Thin as a needle
Small as a mouse

Oh, the sun comes up
And you make a straight line
And you make yourself into a triangle.
Then you make a tiny box
And you grow up like a flower once again.

Oh, the sun goes down
And you spin yourself around
And you make yourself into three triangles.
Then you make a crazy shape
And you melt down like an ice cream cone.

Do Your Own Dance

This dance is self-explanatory. By following the voice prompts, children perform non-locomotor actions, which can also be done as locomotor movements. The dance alternates between action and shape making.

Objective

★ To practice non-locomotor and/or locomotor movement with high and low shape transitions

Activity Basics

1. Play the song for your students and follow the guided CD track. The actions and shapes are as follows:

   First set: jumping, twisting, hopping, and turning

   Second set: twirling, step hopping, melting, and pop-pop-popping up!

   Shapes: big and high, and small and low shapes

   The guided track gives the prompt, "Stop where you are," which signals the shape-making section will begin.

2. At the end of the dance, the prompt is to "balance on one leg and fly." Children can fly from high to low on their spots, or travel to another formation such as a group circle or a single-file line. Be sure to front-load your expectations for the flying by showing students where you want them to end in the space and by modeling safe flying techniques to get there. See the DVD Commentary for more tips.

3. I recommend following this activity with Mountain Breathing (see Body Shapes for Learning on page 55 and Mountain Breathing on the DVD in the Tips and Tricks section) before asking the Reflection questions.

Reflection

Ask the following questions and elicit the following movement to check for understanding:

★ What sharp movements did we make? What smooth movements did we make?

★ Show me a big and high shape. Show me a small and low shape.

★ Show me a body shape balanced on one leg.

CD Tracks
- **9** Guided
- **30** Instrumental

DVD Options
- Traveling version
- Self-space version and transition tip

DVD Commentary
In the Traveling version, children fly out of the space. I used the phrase "Fly away" which was unspecific. I recommend front-loading the ending formation, slowing and clearing, and checking for understanding before you do the activity, so that children end where you want them and use body control, soft focus, and concentration to get there. See Tips and Tricks on the DVD to learn more about these skills.

Concepts

Dance	*Music*	*Physical Education*	*Early Childhood*
Space: self and general space, levels, size	Mood	**Space:** self and general space, levels, size	Physical Development
Body: shape	Tempo	**Body:** shape	
Energy			

Do Your Own Dance

Start where you are, make a shape big and high.

Reach your arms wide. Stretch to the sky.

Now…do your own dance.

Do a jumping dance. Do a twisting dance.

Do a hopping dance. Do a turning dance.

End in a spot. Make yourself small and low.

Shrink on down to a shape just so.

Now, stretch up tall; make a shape, big and high.

And…do your own dance.

Do a twirling dance. Do a step-hop dance.

Do a melting dance. Do a pop-pop-pop dance.

End in a spot. Make a shape big and high.

Take one leg off the floor, can you balance? Now…fly!

Right and Left Hands

Do you want to focus on one direction only? Then, move one hand only and don't move the other hand! You can do this with your youngest students. Before you start, make sure that you, the leader, can reverse right and left when facing the group! Otherwise, you will have to face in the same line of direction as the children.

Objective

★ To develop understanding of right and left

Activity Basics

1. Have the children face you or, if you are comfortable, position yourself in front of the class, facing the same direction as your students (your back will be to them).

2. Play the guided CD track, leading your students through the song. You can "touch the sky" by reaching (from seated position) or jumping (from standing). "Pound" can be performed with one fist pounding into an open hand, onto the other clenched fist, or on the ground.

Going Further

★ Teach left and right with other strategies and then reinforce the concept with this song.

★ To help your students remember which hand is their right hand, consider using this phrase: "Most people write with their right hand."

★ To help with the identifying their left hands, show them that the left hand makes a capital "L" with palm facing away/thumb out perpendicular to the four fingers.

Reflection

Check for understanding by asking your students to do the following things:

★ Tap your left foot.
★ Put your right hand on your head.
★ Shrug your left shoulder.
★ Place your right hand over your heart (useful for learning the Pledge of Allegiance).
★ Reach your left hand up.
★ Flap your right elbow.

CD Tracks
- ⑩ Guided
- ㉓ Instrumental

DVD Option
- Instruction & Demonstration

DVD Commentary
Because this group demonstrated that they could maintain self-control, I risked facing away from the children to practice right and left body parts. If that is not an option for you, face the group to practice isolated body parts as you review and check for understanding. You'll have to reverse your own right and left.

Concepts

Dance
Body: relationships

Physical Education
Motor skills and movement patterns

Early Childhood
Math
Physical Development

Right and Left Hands

This is my right hand, I hold it up high.

This is my left hand, I touch the sky.

Right hand, left hand, roll them all around.

Left hand, right hand, pound, pound, pound!

This is my right hand, I hold it up high.

This is my left hand, I touch the sky.

Galloping Song

Objective
★ To identify and demonstrate the skill of gallop

Activity Basics
1. Form a talking circle and engage your students in a guessing game about what type of movement you are thinking about. In this case, it is a gallop. Provide clues such as clapping the pattern and giving clues about what makes the movement and what letter it begins with. See the video for demonstration.

 One foot leads, the other chases, as you go to different places.

2. Have one child demonstrate how to gallop around the inside of the circle and then allow all students to practice galloping around the circle.

3. Play the guided CD track, galloping to the beat. Halfway through the song, change your leading leg. Cool down to a walk on "walking home" and bring your pony back to the stable to regroup in a circle at the end of the song.

4. Note that the CD track has a short break and then the dance repeats. The same group could do the activity twice or consider dividing the large group into two smaller ones and they can take turns. See Going Further for suggestions on this variation.

5. Once the activity has come to an end, move to the Reflection questions.

Going Further
★ Depending on the size and age of your children, have one set sit in the middle of the circle or around the perimeter while the other travels. After the first time through the song, trade places (with body control) at the pause. To trade places:

  1. Direct the sitters to stand.

  2. The two groups trade places and then the the group that finished sits and does Mountain Breathing, described on page 55 while the other group gallops.

  At the end of the song, give the group that just traveled time to breathe as you move on to the reflection questions.

★ Allow for passing so children who really want to step out are not hampered by the single-file line.

CD Tracks
- ⑪ Guided
- ㉛ Instrumental

DVD Option
- Instruction & Demonstration

DVD Commentary
When the children asked what we would do when it was time for the ponies to rest, I said, "We'll see." I wanted to keep the activity going at that point. It could, however, have been a creative opportunity to activate imagination and share ideas. Keep extension ideas in mind for another day. You can easily layer dramatic play into this motor-skill activity without losing the pace of the lesson by saying, "How/where should the ponies rest today?" This also models multiple solutions and points of view, helping your children to learn how to adapt to change and variation.

- ★ Really get into the imaginative play and pretend you are holding reins, taking the horses out for a gallop and back to the barn.
- ★ For a higher challenge level, change directions and gallop the other way. Vary pathways through the space.

Reflection

- ★ Clap the rhythm of a gallop, and then ask, "What other locomotor movements can we do to this rhythm?" (Skip, side slide)

Concepts

Dance
Space: pathway, direction
Time: pulse, pattern
Locomotor movement skill: galloping

Music
Pulse
Uneven rhythms
Tempo

Physical Education
Motor skill: galloping

Early Childhood
Fine Arts
Language Arts
Physical Development

Galloping Song

See the pony galloping, galloping
All the way to town.

See the pony galloping, galloping
All the way to town.

See the pony galloping, galloping
All the way to town.

See the pony walking home
All tired out, all tired out, all tired out.

Skipping Song

Skipping can be challenging. Children will acquire proficiency at different times and will perform the actions of the song at their differing ability levels. Watch for the children who could benefit from a little one-on-one and skip near them.

CD Tracks
- ⓬ Guided
- ㉜ Instrumental

DVD Option
- Instruction & Demonstration

DVD Commentary
See page 34

Objective

★ To identify and demonstrate the parts of a skip

Activity Basics

1. Form a talking circle and engage your students in a guessing game about what type of movement you are thinking about. In this case, it is a skip. Provide clues such as clapping the pattern of a skip and giving clues about what letter sounds the movement begins with. See the video for demonstration.

2. Ask a student to demonstrate skipping. Point out that each foot has two jobs: a scoop and a chug. Then you change to the other foot. Watch the DVD for a clear demonstration of this.

3. Play the guided CD track and follow the instruction. Work in a circle first. After that, offer the option of moving in free space, but still traveling in the same line of direction.

Going Further

★ For a higher level of challenge, skip backwards. Always start with the scoop.

★ For those needing help, hold hands.

Reflection

Clap the rhythm of a skip, and then ask, "What locomotor movement did we do to that rhythm?" Ask, "What are the two parts of a skip?" (Scoop, chug)

DVD Options

Notice how I gave positive reinforcement even though my younger students did not demonstrate mastery. A typical developmental progression for a child is to have the "scoop-chug" on one foot only before they get the alternating pattern.

Sometimes, when I hold one child's hand to give personal instruction, other children will take hands with a friend because they see it modeled by me. How do you feel about this? My feeling is that as long as the children are succeeding and using body control, it's not a problem. I keep an eye out and terminate the option if I see children pairing up and clowning around by saying "I'm doing this with _____, but I'd like you to skip by yourselves."

Concepts

Dance	*Music*	*Physical Education*	*Early Childhood*
Space: pathway, direction	Pulse	**Motor skill:** skipping	Fine Arts
Time: pulse, pattern	Tempo		Language Arts
Locomotor movement skill: skipping	Uneven rhythms		Physical Development

Skipping Song

Step on one foot, hop on that foot.

Step on the other foot, hop on that foot.

Step on the first foot, hop on that foot,

As I sing this song.

Step-hop …

Skipping, skipping … now let's take a rest.

Walking Song*

Objectives

★ To perform rhyming phrases combining locomotor and non-locomotor movement

★ To learn and practice six basic locomotor movements: walk, hop, slide, jump, skip, and run

★ To learn and practice the skill of turning as a locomotor or non-locomotor movement

Activity Basics

1. Form a talking circle, with ample space in the middle. Ask individuals to model different locomotor movements featured in the song, traveling around the inside of the circle, so that all can see, and back to their spot. The movement groupings are:

   Walk, hop, run, stop

   Slide, jump, run, bump

   March, skip, run, tip

   Turn, creep, run, sleep

   Some things to keep in mind:

   A hop is on one leg, a jump is on two.

   Alternate feet on the hops (three hops and a rest/reverse).

   Slide is a sideways gallop.

   Bump can be a big hip swing from side to side.

   Tip can be a teeter-totter tilt, balancing on one leg on one side and then the other.

   Keep the runs vertical, vigorous, and (depending on the body control of the group and the size of the space) in place!

2. Play the recording and follow the prompts as they are given. Move in time to the music. Follow the rhythm and pulse of the song.

Going Further

★ You can ask older students to identify and model movements that begin with different letter sounds. For example,

   "I'm thinking of a movement that goes from one place to another that uses the "w" sound ... walk!"

   Watch the DVD for detailed modeling of this strategy.

CD Tracks
- ⑬ Guided
- ㉝ Instrumental

DVD Options
- Instruction & Demonstration
- Demonstration

DVD Commentary
While sitting in a talking circle, I front-load all the movements.

Notice how I teach through "I model, you copy" (echo imitation) to assemble the sequence.

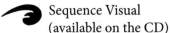 Sequence Visual (available on the CD)

*With thanks to Anne Green Gilbert, who generously granted permission to share this creative approach to a traditional idea.

- ★ When you teach this song, give the verbal cue for the next action during the last two beats of the measure before the transition. The guided track does this for you.
- ★ If your students get dizzy after turning, here's a tip to help:
    The Undizzy Trick: If you need to get undizzy quickly, hold up your pointer finger in front of you and focus on it.
- ★ When traveling through the space, use soft focus. Look for the empty spaces, always seeing, never bumping.
- ★ If traveling around a circle, allow for passing.

 Be a silent potato, eyes everywhere but no mouth!

- ★ Take a deep breath between repetitions of the song.
- ★ For a more challenging experience, front-load all the sequences for all the verses at the beginning, then do the whole dance as demonstrated on the DVD.
- ★ For a less challenging experience, front-load only one sequence. Do that one and then pause the music. Practice the next sequence and then do it with music. Repeat the process for the last two sequences.
- ★ You can also front-load while the students are in scattered space, with one student demonstrator moving among the others. Choose demonstrators based on the following criteria:

    Success for high-need students

    One-on-one attention (such as the side-slide demonstration on the DVD)

    Expectation of good modeling of a more challenging idea (such as skipping)

- ★ Consider creating a visual support by making a poster with images and words that represent the four parts of each sequence so that everyone can read the dance. (One such visual is provided on the CD.)

Reflection

Ask and discuss the following:

- ★ What movements did we do today?
- ★ Which was fastest? Slowest? On one foot?
- ★ What rhyming words did you hear?

Concepts

Dance	Music	Physical Education	Early Childhood
Space: self and general space, direction, pathway, levels	Tempo	Motor skills and movement patterns in a sequence	Fine Arts
	Pulse		Language Arts
Time: speed, pattern			Physical Development
Body: balance			Math
Energy			

Walking Song

Let's walk, hop, run, and stop.

Walking, walking, walking, walking

Hop, hop, hop, hop, hop, hop

Running, running, running, running, running, running

Now we stop. Now we stop.

Next, we'll march, skip, run, and tip.

Marching, marching, marching, marching

Skip, skip, skip, skip, skip, skip

Running, running, running, running, running, running

Tip and tip, tip and tip

Now, we'll slide, jump, run, and bump.

Sliding, sliding, sliding, sliding

Jump, jump, jump, jump, jump, jump

Running, running, running, running, running, running

Bump, bump, bump, bump, bump, bump

Finally, we'll turn, creep, run, and sleep.

Turning, turning, turning, turning

Creep, creep, creep, creep, creep, creep

Running, running, running, running, running, running

Now we sleep. Now we sleep.

Here We Go 'Round and 'Round

CD Tracks
- 14 Guided
- 34 Instrumental

DVD Options
- Sequencing body parts
- Side sliding in a circle
- Two examples

DVD Commentary
In the Sequencing body parts video, notice how I model with description and then repeat in silence to build the sequence.

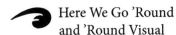
Here We Go 'Round and 'Round Visual

This dance follows an AB form, blending elements of "Here We Go Looby Loo" and the "Hokey Pokey." Teach it to develop the skill of moving as a group around the circle line and emphasizing individual body parts.

Objective
★ To perform a simple AB circle dance using different parts of the body

Activity Basics (Older Students)

1. Invite your students to spread out to a perfect spot and face you to learn the sequence of movements.

2. First, teach the B section (which is essentially the "Hokey Pokey"), beginning with the first body part (head) and then progressing through each of the following body parts in this order: arms, legs, whole self. Use the lyrics as you guide your class through each part of the sequence. As each new body part is added to the sequence, go back to the beginning (head) and perform the entire sequence in silence so that your students will memorize the pattern.

    When you put your whole self in, remember: two legs leave the floor and two legs land.

3. Once the B section is secure, prepare for the A section by having the class sit in ready position in one, large circle or several smaller circles.

4. Model the side slide, traveling around the inside of the circle to show the step. Clearly point out the line of direction by pointing and then by modeling.

5. Using a small group of student demonstrators, model the correct way to hold hands for a side slide. Explain that the children should keep their shoulder blades down and hold hands low. Their shoulders should be over their hips.

    Keep your arms in a "V" shape with people on either side of you, not "H."
   Don't leave your behind behind.

6. Next, practice the side slide with the group as you sing the lyrics, stopping on the word "day" at the end of the phrase, "all on a beautiful day." At the end of the phrase, students should drop hands and face the center of the circle in preparation for the B section.

 The stop is like the period at the end of a sentence.

7. Perform the dance, alternating between the A section and the B section. Drop hands to perform the B section and take hands during the transition back to the A section.

Activity Basics (Younger Children)

1. Form a standing circle.

2. Model the line of direction for traveling around the circle by gesturing in the line of direction.

3. Ask the students to walk around the circle line, with or without holding hands. Stop.

4. Tell them that they will stop after they hear "all on a beautiful day." Emphasize that they will stop right after the word "day."

5. Practice walking and stopping as you sing the A section of the song, cueing the movement.

6. For the B section, improvise moving the body parts into and out of the circle.

7. At the end of the song, freeze in a body shape.

Going Further

★ If walking around the circle line is too challenging, replace traveling with turning in place during "Here we go 'round and 'round," as modeled on the DVD.

★ Put slow learners and disruptive children on either side of you.

★ Intersperse energetic and calm children.

★ Gather ideas for different actions on later repetitions of the dance. In later repetitions, you could include gallop or skip. Small groups can choreograph their own versions!

★ Create a visual support by making a poster with the AB pattern and all the body parts sequenced in order (or use the digital file provided on the CD) to help you and the students learn, review, and remember the dance.

Reflection

Discuss the following questions:

- ★ What kind of locomotor (traveling) movements did we do? (Side slide, walk, jump)
- ★ What kinds of movement did we do on our spot? (Turning, arms, leg and head movements)
- ★ How did we move our head? Arms? Legs? Whole body?
- ★ How did we use body control in the side slides? ("V" arms; no "behind behind"; knowing when to stop after the word day; did not pull or fall down on purpose)

Concepts

Dance	Music	Physical Education	Early Childhood
Space: self and general space, direction	AB form	**Motor skill:** side sliding	Physical Development
Body: parts	Pulse	Body parts	Social & Emotional Development
Time: AB pattern, pulse		Space and relationships	
		Social behavior	

Here We Go 'Round and 'Round

Here we go 'round and 'round,
Here we go 'round and 'round,
Here we go 'round and 'round,
All on a beautiful day.

Let's put our head in,
Let's put our head out,
Let's give our head a SHAKE,
And turn ourselves about.
(Repeat A section.)

Let's put our arm in,
Let's put our arm out,
Let's give our arm a SHAKE,
And turn ourselves about.
(Repeat A section.)

Let's put our leg in,
Let's put our leg out,
Let's give our leg a SHAKE,
And turn ourselves about.
(Repeat A section.)

Let's put our whole selves in,
Let's put our whole selves out,
Let's give ourselves a SHAKE,
And turn ourselves about.
(Repeat A section.)

A Trip to the Zoo

Objective
★ To explore contrasts of speed through imaginative play

Activity Basics

1. Divide the space into two distinct "lands" and mark the transition space between these lands with props, such as cones, yoga squares, or poly spots.

2. Move your students to the transition space, sitting in ready position. Decide which side of the space will be slow land, and which fast land. (Hint: If one side is a smaller or more contained space, make that fast land to help keep students more contained.)

3. Begin to name animals in the song, asking the children to point to the land, slow or fast, that is appropriate for the animal. Use the animal pictures as visual aids and try to break up a predictable slow-fast pattern. In the song, the slow animals are: tortoise, sloth, and elephant. The fast animals are: monkey, cheetah, and little fish in an aquarium. When you introduce the animals, there may be a difference of opinion as to which are fast or slow. This offers the valuable opportunity for discussion and choice.

CD Tracks
- ⓯ Guided
- ㉟ Instrumental

DVD Option
- Instruction & Demonstration

DVD Commentary
If you've divided the space with props, you can designate who will help clean up and where the props will go. You can use this as a reward for cooperation during the activity or to spotlight high-need students.

🐦 Animal Visuals (available on the CD)

4. Explain to your students that you will be playing a song about visiting a zoo and all of the animals that they will see. Instruct the children that upon hearing an animal mentioned in the song, they should travel to the appropriate fast or slow land and dance as that animal in the space. There is also a "free choice" animal. When it comes up, students can go to either side and act out an animal of their choosing. This section is not a free-for-all, but a chance for personal choice and creative expression. You can choose to tell your students about the "free choice" animal

before playing the song or you can pause the music and ask some students for animal suggestions. The song ends with a "heading back," which you can use as a transition to cleaning up and/or establishing another formation, such as lining up at the door or returning to a group circle. Plan for this and alert your students.

5. Play the recording, monitoring behavior and using "I see …" statements to encourage variety. Following the activity, reflect on the experience as time allows.

Going Further

★ Consider doing the activity in place. Children listen, decide on the speed of the animal, and dance on their spots.

★ Do the activity without center cones. Children stop in their own space at each transition, and move through free space at different speeds. Before you begin a free space activity, be sure to review and enforce rules for moving through general space as suggested in the Tips and Tricks section on the DVD.

Reflection

Consider the following as a reflection:

★ What animals did we pretend to be?

★ Show me or tell me about a fast animal or a slow animal.

★ What animal did you pretend to be during free choice? Show me or tell me about your choice.

Concepts

Dance	*Music*	**Physical Education**	**Early Childhood**
Time: speed	Tempo	Speed	Math
Body: shapes		Self-expression	Social & Emotional Development

A Trip to the Zoo

Let's take a trip to the zoo and visit the animals that move slowly and quickly.

We're at the elephant house…

The elephants in the zoo are slow.

The elephants in the zoo are slow.

With great big ears and trunk so low,

The elephants in the zoo are slow.

Now we're at the monkey house…

The monkeys in the zoo are fast.

The monkeys in the zoo are fast.

They hop and swing and have a blast.

The monkeys in the zoo are fast.

Look at those tortoises…

The tortoise in the zoo is slow.

The tortoise in the zoo is slow.

He lives a long time, a hundred years or so,

The tortoise in the zoo is slow.

Let's visit the aquarium…

The little fish in the zoo are fast.

The little fish in the zoo are fast.

They dart through the coral in a tank of glass,

The little fish in the zoo are fast.

How about the rainforest room… What's that up in those trees? It's a sloth!

The big sloth in the zoo is slow.

The big sloth in the zoo is slow.

He hangs around on claws and toes.

The big sloth in the zoo is slow.

Do you want to see the big cats now? Here's one…

The cheetah in the zoo is fast.

The cheetah in the zoo is fast.

He slips away to hide at last,

The cheetah in the zoo is fast.

Let's take a look at one more animal. What is it? You decide!

(Music)

Well…that's all we have time for, so let's head back.

(Whistling)

Our trip is done; it's time to go.

Goodbye to the animals, fast and slow.

Popcorn and Melted Butter

Objective

★ To perform movements with contrasting qualities

Activity Basics

1. Prepare your students for the activity with the following script, showing the movements indicated:

We are going to focus on three movement qualities (also called "energies") in this activity: smooth, sharp, and shaky. Each of these words starts with the letter "S." When you do smooth movement, it is like spreading peanut butter. Let's spread a big "S" in front of us and say "smooth." Sharp movement is like a robot. Let's chop a big "S" in front of us and say "sharp." Shaky movement is wiggly and jiggles around. Let's shake a big "S" in front of us and say "shaky."

2. Instruct the student to find a perfect spot and stand tall.

3. Play the music, following along with the prompts as they are given. Remind your students to "Stay on their spot" (if you do the activity in place) or "Move into the empty spaces, so you don't get hurt"(if you travel).

4. Following the activity, move to a talking circle or seated position to reflect on the experience.

Reflection

★ What movements were smooth? (Melted butter, floating clouds, maybe squirmy snakes)

★ What movements were sharp? (Popcorn, jumping beans)

★ What movements were shaky? (Jell-O™, maybe squirmy snakes)

CD Tracks
- 16 Guided
- 36 Instrumental

DVD Option
- Instruction & Demonstration

DVD Commentary
Notice how we hold the "freeze" during the transitions. We model a traveling version, but the children basically stay in one place in the demonstration. It would be easy to keep this whole activity in one spot.

Concepts

Dance	***Music***	***Physical Education***	***Early Childhood***
Energy: smooth, sharp, shaky	Tempo	Energy	Math
	Expression	Self-expression	
	Articulation		

Popcorn and Melted Butter

Let's move like popcorn, and melted butter.

Popcorn! Melted butter

Popcorn! Melted butter

Popcorn! Melted butter

Popcorn…

Pop!

Now let's move like jumping beans and squirmy snakes.

Jumping beans! Squirmy snakes!

Popcorn …

Pop!

Time for Jell-O™ and floating clouds.

Jell-O! Floating clouds.

Popcorn…

Pop!

Old MacDonald Had a Farm

We were inspired to create this version of the song when we were helping young children describe the sounds of percussion instruments. In this activity, children name the animals and sounds they hear.

CD Track
17 Guided

DVD Commentary
This is the only performance segment. Everyone can watch and enjoy. What are the animals? You decide!

Objectives
- ★ To sharpen listening skills and imagination
- ★ To stimulate curiosity

Activity Basics
1. Show your students an assortment of interesting percussion instruments, including pitched and non-pitched.
2. Play the instruments for the students and ask them to describe the sounds they hear, and what the sound makes them think of.
3. Watch the video.
4. Create your own version, using the instruments you have.

Going Further
- ★ Challenge the students to create found sounds or categorize instruments into family groups (wood, metal, skin).
- ★ Add movement and gesture to the sounds.
- ★ Find a storybook version of the song and assign characters to different students. Bring the book to life through sound and movement.

Reflection
Ask your students:
- ★ What instruments did you hear? What did they sound like to you? Why?

Concepts

Dance	Music	Physical Education	Early Childhood
Make connections between dance and other disciplines (music)	Verse/Refrain Timbre	Tempo Self-expression	Language Arts Fine Arts Social & Emotional Development

Free Dance

CD Track
🔘 18 Instrumental

DVD Options
- Instruction & Demonstration
- Obstacle course variations

This multipurpose, instrumental arrangement is a useful piece for a lot of different activities and to address any number of objectives and concepts.

Activity Basics

Use this track for any of the following fun activities:

★ Playing a dance game by having one or more students take turns free dancing in the center of a circle while everyone else imitates the child's movements or just dances along

★ Practicing locomotor movement

★ Going through a movement obstacle course (such as leaping over or traveling under and through)

★ Dancing in scattered space to explore pathways, relationships, and direction in space

★ Free dancing, with or without props, before class begins (in a studio setting) or as a "dance break"

★ Doing your own thing. The sky's the limit!

DVD Commentary

In the first segment, free dance variations flow from one idea to another. They include the dance game with children coming into the center, free dancing with and without props, and traveling across the floor one by one. The obstacle course variation is a detailed modeling of two different courses. The first is great for practicing leaping, taking turns, and starting/ending from a moving line. The second is an exploration of relationships in space (the "preposition places," such as over, under, and on). It is also a great way to build language vocabulary and spatial awareness.

Notice how we talk about a gatekeeper who opens the gate to let the next student begin. This keeps the line moving which cuts down on restlessness and impatience. Bring the next student into the course once the previous person has gone a safe distance.

Concepts

Dance	Music	Physical Education	Early Childhood
Space: pathways, directions	Steady Beat	Motor skills	Fine Arts
Body: relationships	Form	Social behavior	Social & Emotional Development
Time: pulse			

Little Birdies

Objectives

★ To respond to visual and auditory cues
★ To move cooperatively through the space
★ To engage imagination
★ To introduce a spanking run

CD Tracks
⑲ Guided
㊲ Instrumental

DVD Option
- Instruction & Demonstration

DVD Commentary
After I tap the birdies to wake them up, I crouch to the level of the children. By doing this, I can model a slow rise to standing as well as the line of direction in which they should fly, making the amount of flying time just right. Also notice how I ask the children to practice flying again since they do such a messy job the first time. This models expectations for following directions accurately.

Activity Basics

1. Model the sleeping birdie shape: knees down, seat on feet, nose to knees. Have everyone make the shape.

2. Explain that when the grown up bird taps someone on the back, that means "Wake up, little birdie!"

3. With everyone seated in ready position, model the three characteristic of the flying movement around the outside of the circle. The characteristics are:

    Wide wings: outstretched arms, not flapping

    Spanking run: feet brush off the floor (brushing-back feet), swiping back on every step, toes try to touch your bottom

    A light and buoyant center

 You'll be the watchers and I'll be the doer.

4. Return to your place in the circle and invite the students to stand tall. Guide your students to practice flying with the characteristics you have modeled. Fly once around and stop when everyone is back to their starting spot. Instruct the children to fly once around, return to the circle, and sit in ready position.

5. Prepare for the ending of the activity by standing in the middle of the circle and making a "come here" gesture with your hands. Ask your students, "What does this movement mean? That's right, come here!" Explain that when you play the music, you will go back to the nest a little before the children. When they see the gesture, they should turn, fly back to the nest, and go to sleep. Model this sequence of events by flying straight to the nest and going back into the sleeping shape as you explain your actions.

6. Perform the dance with the guided CD track.

Going Further

★ Students must commit to rules for safe flying and returning to the nest. Hold the hand of a student that feels he/she cannot comply, or allow that student to sit out and watch once. You might also, while flying, swoop down on unsafe fliers, hold their hand and fly with them. Share the following rules for safe flying:

> Fly in the line of direction that the grown up bird indicates through gesture.
>
> Use the spanking run and body control.
>
> Fly safely back to the nest; come into the nearest place when the grown up bird gestures "come here."

★ Students who cannot fly safely may be "bird watchers," sitting out and using their "binoculars" to watch. This is not a punishment, but an alternative and a chance to see how the activity is done.

★ You can also have two groups: bird watchers and birds. Switch roles so that all have a chance to experience both roles. See the DVD for an example of this transition.

Reflection

Ask the children:

★ What was the sleeping shape?
★ How did we fly?
★ How did you know in which direction to fly?
★ What was the gesture for "come here"?
★ What did you do when you saw the "come here" gesture?
★ What kind of bird were you?

Concepts

Dance	Music	Physical Education	Early Childhood
Space: self and general space, direction, pathway, levels	Tempo	**Motor skill:** spanking run	Physical Development
	Expression	Self-expression	
Body: parts, relationships		Social behavior	

Little Birdies

All the little birdies were sleeping in their nest.
All the little birdies were taking a rest.
They didn't even twitter and they didn't even tweet!
Everything was quiet, up and down the street.

Along came the grown up bird and tapped them on their heads.
They opened up their little eyes, and stretched their wings up to the sky,
And this is what it said,

"Come little birdies, it's time to learn to fly.
Come little birdies, 'way up in the sky.
Now fly, fly, fly away, fly, fly, fly.
Fly, fly, fly away, 'way up in the sky.
Fly, fly, fly away, birdies fly the BEST.
Fly, fly, fly away, now fly back to your nest."

This activity was adapted from the poem "Little Birdies" found in *Creative Movement for the Developing Child* by Clare Cherry and used with the generous permission of her heirs.

Resting

We often forget that a moment of complete rest for our muscles and bones can have the same refreshing impact on our bodies and minds as a short nap. Children experience the positive effects of conscious and constructive relaxation combined with deep breathing through this activity.

CD Tracks
- (20) Guided
- (38) Instrumental

DVD Options
- Alignment instruction
- Demonstration

DVD Commentary
I model an alignment adjustment on one student, slowly and in great detail. Notice how quickly I work when adjusting members of the whole group.

Objective
★ To promote body awareness, alignment, and restorative relaxation

Activity Basics

1. Model the resting position: legs slightly apart, arms at the sides of the trunk and slightly apart, at about a 45-degree angle, lengthening along the floor. Let the back of the head be heavy. Take a slow, full, deep breath in through the nose, and slowly out again.

2. As you model the movement, let the children know that they need to be quiet so that everyone can enjoy the peaceful atmosphere without distractions.

3. Demonstrate how to come out of resting: bend one knee and then the other. Cross your arms over your trunk. Roll to your right side. Use your hands to push yourself up to sitting, with your hands in your lap, legs crossed in ready position. If your eyes were closed, slowly open them. Take one more deep breath to end.

4. Play the recording, modeling the movement. You can add the tactile dimension to this activity and model sensory awareness of skeletal alignment by gently lengthening the legs, arms, and back of the head of all, most, or some of the children as they rest. See the DVD for a demonstration.

Going Further
★ Include resting after dynamic activity and before creative time.
★ When a group no longer can focus, resting is a good solution. See also Mountain Breathing in Tips and Tricks on the DVD for a simple way to rest and relax between activities.

Concepts

Dance	Music	Physical Education	Early Childhood
Body awareness	Mood	Health	Physical Development
	Tempo		Social & Emotional Development

Goodbye Song

Objective
★ To leave the space

Activity Basics (Seated Version)
1. Play the recording and wave goodbye with different body parts on different levels and in different spatial relationships.

2. When the music pauses, freeze, smile, wink (or blink), and then wave again.

3. If you wish, have the children stand and dance to the door to line up, return to their tables or desks, put on their shoes, etc. Children could dance to the door one-by-one or grouped by name, color of clothing, birth month, etc.

Activity Basics (Standing Version)
1. In a standing circle, practice wiggling on your spot and freezing on a sound cue (drum, hand clap, or voice).

2. Play the recording and wiggle during the first part of the song.

3. Freeze, smile, wink (or blink) at the pause, and then wiggle again and freeze or transition to shoes, line, desk, etc.

Activity Basics (Traveling Version)
1. Lead the class to travel around the circle line, with or without holding hands, as you sing.

2. Stop to smile and wink.

3. Walk again to finish.

Going Further
★ As the song continues, give the children an opportunity to dance freely on their spots and/or lead them in dancing around the circle and to the door.

★ Play the song at the end of the day as getting-ready-to-leave music while the children put on their coats, boots, etc.

★ For a higher challenge level, do the dance as a side slide around the circle (see "Here We Go 'Round and 'Round" for detailed instructions), stopping to smile and wink, taking hands on "Oh, it's," and resuming the side slide on "time to say goodbye." This is most effective when you break large groups into two or more smaller groups with a strong leader in each group.

★ This song is a great closing activity for a family program too. See the DVD for fun ideas!

CD Tracks
- 21 Guided
- 39 Instrumental

DVD Options
- Seated version
- Standing version
- Parent/child version

DVD Commentary
Notice how the silly waves here are similar to the waves in "Welcome Song." Use that to your advantage!

Reflection

★ What are some funny ways you can wave goodbye?

Concepts

Dance
Space: self and general, pathway, direction
Body: parts (gesture)
Energy: expression

Music
Steady beat
Tempo

Physical Education
Space: pathway, direction
Body: parts (gesture)
Social behavior

Early Childhood
Social & Emotional Development

Goodbye Song

Oh, it's time to say goodbye to everyone.

Oh, it's time to say goodbye to everyone.

Oh, it's time to say goodbye,

Make a smile, and wink an eye,

Oh, it's time to say goodbye to everyone.

Body Shapes for Learning

Body shapes for learning are a shorthand method for cueing spatial transitions for listening, moving, resting, and reflecting. These shapes are very helpful for gathering and organizing students throughout the day, whether calling them to the carpet, lining up, beginning a movement activity, or taking a moment to rest and redirect.

Teach these space management procedures to streamline pacing and manage behavior. The shapes are very specific, and each one carries a set of expectations. They are used in every movement activity. Teach them as you need them, and then refer to them by name.

Body Shape	How to make it	Why and When
Sit Ready Position	Sitting, legs crossed. Say, "Eyes, nose and belly button facing me."	For listening to instructions, observing modeling, and reflecting
		To promote concentration
Stand Tall, One and All	Standing, arms at sides.	To begin movement
		For receiving brief instructions
Talking Circle	Take hands to make a circle round. Drop hands. Sit down in Ready Position.	For all circle activities, group reflection, and brainstorming
Open the Circle	Take a mini/jump/wiggle/crocodile-sized/stiff step back.	To give space to dance inside the circle, travel along the circle line, or move in place with extra space on either side of you
Find a Perfect Spot	Students scatter in the room, doing a "helicopter check" to be sure they are not too near anyone or thing.	For movement that requires a lot of space around each person or leads into traveling
Mountain Breathing	Sit in Ready Position. Touch the top of your head. Tie an imaginary string there. Reach it up to the ceiling and tie it there. Let your hands float down to rest upon your knees. Now, place your fingertips on either side of that imaginary string above your head, elbows back, and shoulders down.	For calming and centering between activities, before reflection, and when concentration needs to be reinstated
		Also useful when setting up or breaking down from an activity
Single-File Line	Leader stands at the head of the line, holding arms forward and parallel to each other and says, "I want to see you between my arms." (And show me all your charms.)	To move across the floor one-by-one
		To enter and leave the space
Go elbow-to-elbow with a partner (or toe-to-toe, back-to-back, wrist-to-wrist, etc.	Connect body parts with another person.	To find a partner for paired activity

Lesson Plan Suggestions

Below are a series of suggested lesson plans. The first two columns represent possible introductory lessons based on your class time. The next four lessons concentrate on a specific target concept. These are: Following Instruction, Language Arts, Sequence & Shapes (Math), and Calming Down.

20-minute Introductory Lesson	30-minute Introductory Lesson	Following Instruction	Language Arts	Sequence & Shape (Math)	Calming Down
Down by the Station (enter)	Down by the Station (enter)	Everybody Do This (one set)	The Welcome Song (with rhyming jump up endings)	Everybody Do This (one set)	Flea Song
The Welcome Song	The Welcome Song	Old MacDonald	Walking Song (with letter sound connections)	Shape Song	Little Birdies
Flea Song	Flea Song	Do Your Own Dance			Resting
Your choice of one or two additional activities	Everybody Do This (one set)	Little Birdies			
Down by the Station (exit)	Your choice of one to three additional activities				
	Down by the Station (exit)				

56 ★ Lesson Plan Suggestions

Early Childhood Concept Index

	Fine Arts	Language Arts	Math	Physical Development	Social & Emotional Development	Social Science
Down by the Station				Demonstrate ability to cooperate with others during group physical activities		
The Welcome Song		Begin to develop phonological awareness by participating in rhyming activities	Show understanding and use comparative words (big/small; high/low, etc.)	Identify body parts and their functions	Exhibit persistence and creativity in seeking solutions to problems (How to wave different ways. How to jump up tall different ways)	
Flea Song				Identify body parts and their functions		
Everybody Do This		Make some letter-sound matches	Count with understanding Recognize patterns	Identify body parts and their functions		Recall information about the immediate past
Shape Song		Understand that reading progresses from left to right and top to bottom Understand that print carries a message Relate prior knowledge to new information Predict what will happen next using pictures and content for guides	Recognize geometric shapes and structures Recognize, duplicate, and extend simple patterns, such as sequences of sounds, shapes, or colors	Coordinate movement to perform complex tasks	Exhibit eagerness and curiosity as a learner Show some initiative and independence in actions	
Do Your Own Dance				Demonstrate ability to cooperate with others during group physical activities		

Early Childhood Concept Index ★ 57

	Fine Arts	Language Arts	Math	Physical Development	Social & Emotional Development	Social Science
Right and Left Hands			Show understanding of and use comparative words	Engage in activity using fine motor skills		
Galloping Song	Rhythmic awareness (an element of music and dance)	Make some letter-sound matches ("g" sound)		Follow simple safety rules while participating in activities		
Skipping Song	Rhythmic awareness (an element of music and dance)	Make some letter-sound matches ("sk" sound)		Follow simple safety rules while participating in activities		
Walking Song	Rhythmic awareness (an element of music and dance)	Make some letter-sound matches	Recognize, duplicate, and extend simple patterns, such as sequences of sounds, shapes, or colors	Follow simple safety rules while participating in activities Coordinate movements to perform complex tasks		
Here We Go 'Round and 'Round				Demonstrate ability to cooperate with others during group physical activities Identify body parts and their functions	Develop relationships with children and adults	
A Trip to the Zoo			Find and name locations with simple words, such as "near" Show understanding and use of comparative words		Show some initiative and independence in actions Begin to understand and follow rules	
Popcorn and Melted Butter			Show understanding and use of comparative words			
Old MacDonald Had a Farm	Describe or respond to the creative work of others	Identify some letters			Exhibit eagerness and curiosity as a learner (when identifying the different animal sounds)	

58 ★ Early Childhood Concept Index

	Fine Arts	Language Arts	Math	Physical Development	Social & Emotional Development	Social Science
Free Dance	Describe and respond to one's own creative work and the creative work of others				Show some initiative and independence in actions	
Little Birdies				Follow simple safety rules while participating in activities		
Resting				Participate in simple practices that promote healthy living and prevent illness	Show empathy and caring for others	
Goodbye Song					Develop relationships with children and adults	

Early Childhood Concept Index ★ 59

Quick Reference Guide

Activity	Page	CD Tracks	
		Guided	**Instrumental**
Down by the Station	9	1	22
The Welcome Song	11	2	23
Flea Song	14	3	24
Everybody Do This	16	4–7	25–28
Shape Song	22	8	29
Do Your Own Dance	27	9	30
Right and Left Hands	29	10	23
Galloping Song	31	11	31
Skipping Song	33	12	32
Walking Song	35	13	33
Here We Go 'Round and 'Round	38	14	34
A Trip to the Zoo	41	15	35
Popcorn and Melted Butter	45	16	36
Old MacDonald Had a Farm	47	17	
Free Dance	48	18	
Little Birdies	49	19	37
Resting	52	20	38
Goodbye Song	53	21	39